Contents

Overview	3
Top 10 experiences in Argentina	3
Climate and weather	5
Where to stay	6
Getting around	7
Eating in Argentina	9
Cultural highlights and etiquette	10
Safety and scams	12
LGBTQ travel	13
Visas and vaccinations	14
Buenos Aires and Surrounds	15
Local's guide to Buenos Aires	16
Nightlife	19
Day Trips from Buenos Aires	20
The North	21
Northeast Argentina	22
The Northwest	24
Central Argentina	26
Central Sierras	27
The Midwest: Mendoza and beyond	29

Patagonia	31
The Lake District	32
Southwest Patagonia	35
Coastal Patagonia	37
Tierra del Fuego	39
Outdoor Adventure	40
Hiking and trekking	41
Winter sports	43
Rafting, kayaking, and diving	44
Camping	45
Where to see wildlife	46
Best road trips	48
Off the beaten path	50
Essential Insurance Tips	52
Our contributors	55
See our other guides	55
Need an insurance quote?	56

Welcome!

Argentina is tango, the Fitz Roy trek, and the thundering Iguazu Falls – but it's also cloud forests, Welsh villages, and volcanic deserts. Vast in scale, and scenic beyond belief, this South American nation offers an infinite variety of adventures, from gaucho culture in the north to penguin-spotting in the south.

Our Insiders' Picks of Argentina's Top 10 Experiences

Hang out with penguins on the Patagonian coast

Punta Tumbo is home to the largest colony of Magellanic penguins in South America. During nesting season (September-March) the beach is a-waddle with some 500,000 birds. Keep your eyes open for the other black and white residents of the area – killer whales.

Traditional *asado*

Indulge in a traditional Argentine barbecue

A trip to Argentina isn't complete without experiencing the national dish: *asado* (grilled meat). The cut of meat determines the price – the region determines whether it's beef, lamb, pork, or even venison, llama, or goat, being grilled up. If you're a vegetarian, don't fear – the side dishes are meals all by themselves.

Keep it surreal in Salta and Mendoza

From the blindingly white flats of the Salinas Grandes and the strangely shaped, polychromatic rock formations of the Quebradas de Humahuaca, to the lunar expanse of La Payunia's black, volcanic desert, it's easy to feel you're on another planet.

Get a taste of history at a *bodegon*

Buenos Aires offers all kinds of modern, gourmet, and international food, but for a true local's experience, seek out the *bodegones*. These are traditional, family-style restaurants that have often been in the same location for decades – places with hand-painted detailing on the windows, old newspaper clippings on the walls, and ceilings hung with legs of ham and quirky chandeliers.

Hike to a glacial lake

Argentine Patagonia is studded with alpine lakes of every shade, from jade green to icy blue to deep sapphire. Trek to iconic Laguna de los Tres, with its magnificent views of Mount Fitz Roy, or choose one of the lesser-known trails and discover your own private lagoon.

Ski at the world's southernmost resort

Cerro Castor, in Tierra del Fuego National Park, doesn't have the fame of Las Leñas or Cerro Catedral – and that's part of its appeal. With fantastic powder and few crowds, this gem of a resort is worth a journey to (almost) the ends of the earth.

Sip Malbec at the world's highest vineyards

Argentina's Mendoza region is famous for award-winning wineries surrounded by snowy Andean peaks. But if you want to sample wine grown at the highest elevation anywhere, head to the Calchaqui Valley in the northwest, where you'll find vineyards at a dizzying 9,842ft (3,000m).

land-sailing at Barreal Blanco

> **This dry lakebed in San Juan Province gets winds of more than 75mph (120kph), perfect for the thrilling sport of *carrovelismo*.**

Discover a slice of Europe

Argentina is a country of immigrants, and there are traces of international influence everywhere. When you're sipping tea and sampling cakes at a Welsh teahouse in Gaiman, or drinking German beer in the Bavarian-style hamlet of La Cumbresita, you might forget you're in South America for a moment.

Try land-sailing at Barreal Blanco

This dry lakebed in San Juan Province gets winds of more than 75mph (120kph), perfect for the thrilling sport of *carrovelismo* – like windsurfing, but on land. Once you've zipped your way across the plains, go stargazing at the nearby Complejo Astronómico El Leoncito – the skies in this area are clear 300 nights a year.

Dive into folklore culture at a *peña*

There's more to Argentine dance than tango. In the North, gauchos take the floor at boisterous folk music parties that blend Spanish and indigenous traditions. Spectators are highly encouraged to join in.

Climate and Weather

Spanning almost 2,490mi (4,000km) in length, Argentina's terrain is as varied as its climate, and those regional variations will play a big role in determining the best time to travel around the country.

Autumn in Patagonia

Summer
December through February are the busiest months for travel to Argentina. In sub-antarctic Patagonia and Tierra del Fuego, you can expect the average temperature to hover around 59°F (15°C) – in the Lake District, around 70°F (20°C). However, these months also bring hordes of visitors, so you'll need to book in advance for hotels and campsites and expect more people on the trails.

This is also the only time frame when you can expect to climb Aconcagua, the highest peak outside of Asia, found in the Mendoza region.

It's worth noting that while this is the most popular season to visit the southern regions of Argentina, summer brings high temperatures, rain, and consequent flooding to the north, making autumn and spring better for exploring that region. If you prefer not to swelter, best to steer clear of Buenos Aires during the summer, too.

Autumn
March, April, and May are the perfect time for wine lovers to visit the midwestern provinces of Mendoza and San Juan for the wine harvest. Early autumn is also ideal for seeing fall foliage in the Lake District, Southern Patagonia, and Tierra del Fuego. Weather can be unpredictable this time of year, however, and be aware that Easter is a peak holiday time for locals – hotels and tours can book up quickly.

Winter
June through August is considered low season in Argentina – the exception is the month of July, which is a holiday for many locals. Winter means great skiing at Argentina's many resorts, but heavy snowfall can block many of the hiking trails in Patagonia. This is also the best time to avoid the crowds at Iguazu Falls.

Spring
September through November offer ideal weather across almost the entire country. Visit the capital, Buenos Aires, before the humidity and crowds descend in summer. The Northwest sees milder temperatures around 70°F (20°C). The beaches along the western coastline are less packed this time of year, too.

> **Winter means great skiing at Argentina's many resorts, but heavy snowfall can block many of the hiking trails in Patagonia.**

Where to Stay

In Argentina, you'll be spoiled for choice when it comes to accommodation – from *posadas* and *estancias* to boutique hotels and hostels.

Ecolodge, Mendoza

In bigger cities, like Buenos Aires, Cordoba, and Mendoza, expect a mix of swanky hotels, apartments, budget hostels, and guesthouses. In rural areas and the Lake District, upscale lodging tends to be more boutique-style, or you can stay at *estancias* (ranches turned B&B, also known as *fincas*).

For budget travelers

If you're on a tighter budget, try websites like Airbnb (but beware of Airbnb scams). This is a good option if there's a group of you, as you can rent an entire apartment for far less than a hotel – plus, you can cook for yourselves to save money on dining.

You'll also find hostels with dorm beds starting at US $10 ($262 ARS) per night, and double rooms starting around US $25 ($655 ARS) per night.

For mid-range travelers

Apartments are still a good bet for mid-range travelers, but it's sometimes nice to stay in a guesthouse rather than be secluded in an apartment with no other travelers around.

Have a look at *posadas* (small guest houses with just a few rooms). Many have shared bathrooms, but others have private showers and toilets. Breakfast is typically included, along with a kitchen for your use. Double rooms usually range from US $50-$75 ($1,310-$1,965 ARS) per night.

For a bit of luxury

If you have money burning a hole in your pocket, or just want to experience a different style of accommodation during your trip, consider a lodge, chalet, boutique hotel, or *estancia*.

Estancias are ranches or farms which offer rooms, food, and activities for guests. You'll get to learn about life on the farm and can be as involved as you want. For two people, costs generally run around US $200 ($5,240 ARS) per night.

Mountain lodges (often with stunning views, spas, and restaurants on site) or boutique hotels (often converted family houses, with each room decorated differently) start at around US $115 ($3,015 ARS) per night, and are worth splurging on.

> **Note**
> As of 2017, if you pay for your hotel with your foreign credit card, you no longer have to pay the 21% tax.

Getting Around

From serene alpine lakes to rocky Atlantic beaches, subtropical jungles to the tip of the world, getting around Argentina means covering a lot of ground. Here are the best and most popular modes of transport.

Bus driving through Salta province

Buses

Buses are probably the best way to get around Argentina, and there are numerous bus companies to choose from. You can either go online to book – Omnilineas is a good online booking platform – or show up at the bus station to pre-purchase your tickets there. You'll have the choice of class between *comon* (regular seat), *semi-cama* (seat that reclines part way), *coche cama* (seat that reclines almost all the way flat), and *ejecutivo* (executive sleeper).

The price of the bus journey varies depending on the company and the route. Each bus company is different, and you'll want to note what is included with the bus you choose: food, bathroom, refreshments (wine!), attendants, stops, etc. But to give an example, an overnight, 15-hour journey from Buenos Aires to Mendoza will cost around US $75 ($1,965 ARS). Overnight trips can be a great way to save money on the cost of a hotel.

Flights

Whether or not you choose to fly will depend on your budget (and your tolerance for long bus rides).

A flight from Buenos Aires to Mendoza will cost around US $160 ($4,190 ARS) with LATAM and Aerolineas Airlines – with Aerolineas, you'll have to tack on a further US $80 ($2,095 ARS) for your first checked bag. There's also a new domestic budget airline called Fly Bondi which often has good deals.

Buses tend to cost 50% less than flights – and if you consider that a bus ride counts as an overnight stay, and that you often need to take an

> **Buses tend to cost 50% less than flights – and if you consider that a bus ride counts as an overnight stay, it often ends up being much more economical.**

Road across the Andes

Driving - El Chalten

expensive taxi out to the airport (and in), it often ends up being much more economical to take the bus.

Rental vehicle

Renting a car is a great way to see Argentina at your own pace. Pulling over for picnics, stopping for photos whenever you feel like it, and taking random, scenic side roads is what it's all about.

The only downside is that renting a car will cost you about US $50 ($1,310 ARS) per day. Discounts are sometimes available if you rent for a week or more. Also, you'll want to make sure that you do a loop, so that you can pick up and return the vehicle to the same place. Otherwise, you'll be looking at a huge drop-off fee (typically US $0.60/$16 ARS per km). For example, if you picked up in Mendoza and dropped off in Bariloche, that would cost you a hefty US $720 ($18,865 ARS) drop-off fee!

General Cost Guide

Accommodations

Hostels: Dorm beds starting at US $10 ($262 ARS), double rooms starting around US $25 ($655 ARS)

Lodges and boutique hotels: US $115 ($3,015 ARS)

Posadas, double room: US $50-$75 ($1,310-$1,965 ARS)

Estancias, double room: US $200 ($5,240 ARS)

Dining

Food in Argentina can be very expensive or very cheap, depending on what you eat.

Empanadas (small pies stuffed with meat or cheese) and other fried snack foods only cost about US $1.25 ($33 ARS) each. But living off *empanadas* gets boring after a while. This country is famous for its *parrillas* (steak houses) and even if you're on a strict budget, you have to open your wallet for a juicy ribeye at least once.

The El Calafate region of Patagonia is known for its fire-grilled lamb, which costs around US $18 ($472 ARS) for the meat – sides are extra. Ribeyes in Bariloche cost around $15 ($393 ARS) – sides are extra.

In Buenos Aires, you can find lots of cheaper *parrillas* with steaks and sides for around $10 ($262 ARS). The cut of beef you choose really dictates the price.

Dining at a vineyard around Mendoza or Cafayate is an experience in itself, but you'll spend around US $70 ($1,835 ARS) for the opportunity.

A Menu of the Day at a local restaurant consisting of an appetizer, main, dessert, and drink will usually be around $10 ($262 ARS).

Eating in Argentina

Argentine dishes tend to reflect the surrounding landscapes – fish from the mighty rivers of the Northeast, beef from the grassy Pampas rangelands. Meals start late, and are always accompanied by plenty of conversation.

Empanadas

Traditional food

Number one in Argentina's traditional dishes is *asado* (grilled meat), either on a barbecue or on cross-form metal bars over an open flame. *Asado* gathers family and friends and, depending on the region, different meats are used: beef or pork in the Pampas, mostly lamb in the South, and in the sierras and Northwest it's baby goat. In Patagonia, look for *curanto*, a Polynesia-influenced asado dug into the ground, cooked on hot slabs of stone and covered by brush. Argentine *curanto* features sweet potatoes and apples paired with lamb or venison.

The best wine to pair with *asado* is Malbec, Argentina's internationally known grape.

Other specialties include *empanadas*, small pies stuffed with meat, onions, peppers, olives, and egg. They're usually the starter of a huge *asado*. On Independence Day (July 9), the customary dish is *locro*, a stew made from white corn, pork, beans, and red chorizo.

A typical northwestern delicacy is *humita en chala*, made with milk, fresh corn, onions, spices, and goat cheese, all steamed in corn leaves. *Carbonada*, found around the country in different variations, is a hotpot of corn, meat, onions, peppers, and paprika, served inside a hollow pumpkin previously baked with milk and sugar. The best wine for these dishes is Torrontes, scented with flowers and very intense.

If you're fond of sweets, don't miss *alfajores*: two biscuits joined together with a filling of mousse, *dulce de leche*, or jam and covered with chocolate or powdered sugar.

Modern dining

In larger cities, you'll find many restaurants offering modern takes on traditional dishes, along with international choices ranging from Japanese to Armenian. A new trend in Buenos Aires is the *puerto cerrado* (closed door) restaurant, where dinners are served in a private home or shop, its location kept secret until you make a reservation. They're only open a few nights a week, and the menus change frequently.

> " I recommend that travelers try *bodegones*: traditional restaurants in old buildings. When you go into one, you'll feel like the walls speak.

Andrés Brenner,
Videographer and Buenos Aires local

Cultural Highlights & Etiquette

If you tell an Argentinian that you'll be visiting the country, rest assured that what will come next is: you will be offered a place to stay, invited to a traditional barbeque, asked to go sightseeing with the friend of a friend and, most of all, you will be offered *mate*. Don't even think of saying no!

Mate

The culture of *mate*: sharing is caring

Mate may be the single thing that culturally defines all Argentinians. It's what they do, all day, while doing anything else. The *mate* ritual reflects their most deeply rooted values: sharing and friendship.

This bitter type of tea, known as *Yerba Mate*, is served in a small cup with an aluminium straw that everyone shares by turns.

It goes without saying that for visitors wanting to blend in, it's not a good idea to look disgusted when seeing 10 people drinking from the same straw.

Public affection: a society of hugs and kisses

Argentinians are quite relaxed about public displays of affection, which can sometimes be surprising for foreigners. When greeting someone, Argentinians will give a kiss – only one – on the right cheek, sometimes even a tight hug. This goes for men and women. Talking loudly and with energetic body language is also perfectly okay.

Politics, religion, and football

As a society, Argentinians can be quite polarized by concepts such as politics, military, church, and football. Footballers Maradona and Messi; Malvinas (aka the Falkland Islands); the Pope; Juan and Evita Perón: are all sensitive topics. A simple conversation can turn into an intense debate quite easily, so don't take it personally if you find yourself in the middle!

Apart from *mate*, *asado*, and tango, football is the quintessence of all things Argentine. You don't need to visit the famous stadium in La Boca to get a sense of this: almost every neighborhood has its own football team. The whole country stops for the Sunday games, and it's said that if you want to

> " It goes without saying that for visitors wanting to blend in, it's not a good idea to look disgusted when seeing 10 people drinking from the same straw.

Carnival in Buenos Aires

say you've visited, you have to go to a stadium and see a match.

Going with the flow

Accept the realities of Argentina. You may encounter strikes, demonstrations, people crossing the road on red lights, dog poo, and crowds everywhere (if you're in major cities) on almost a daily basis. This can create a sense of chaos and overwhelm visitors, but don't let it spoil the fun. Try not to be bothered by people not being on time, concerts starting late, or buses being tardy. There's really no reason to rush.

Siestas and dinner

Many regions of the country, especially the hottest ones, follow the custom of *siesta* – napping in the afternoon. You can expect everything to be shut down from 12:30pm until 4-5pm. Locals usually eat dinner around 9 or 10pm. That's why Argentinians eat *merienda* (afternoon tea) around 6pm. This translates to late mornings, so you won't find much open before 10am.

Music and festivals in Argentina

Tango is on UNESCO's Intangible Cultural Heritage list, and it's deeply embedded in the Argentine culture.

But the love for music goes beyond tango. There's also the Cosquín Festival – Argentina's most important folk music festival, held in Cordoba, during January. The festival lasts nine nights and the artists' lineup is always top notch.

And there's the Argentine version of rock 'n' roll: Rock Nacional. One of the best experiences for a visitor is to go to a rock concert, get in the middle of things and jump around like there's no tomorrow – that's called "pogo."

Other major festivals are the *Fiesta de la Vendimia* (Grape Harvest Festival), held February-March in Mendoza, and the extravagant *Carnaval de Gualeguaychu*, which takes place in Entre Ríos mid-January to late March, and is the most famous festival in the country.

These festivals are hugely popular and draw huge crowds. If you go, make sure to plan ahead of time.

8 Must-do Experiences for Travelers

Sit at the park and have *mate* with new friends: just say *"¿Me das un mate?"*

Attend a folklore festival or *peña*

Watch a game of *pato* (the traditional sport of gauchos) at Las Heras in Mendoza

Visit indigenous communities and towns to help keep their heritage alive

Dance tango at a *milonga* (tango venue)

Eat traditional *asado* with the gauchos

Drink wine, of course – but remember to try *Fernet con Coca*. If you tell an Argentinian, especially from Cordoba, that you've tried this, you'll make a friend on the spot.

Listen to *Cuarteto*, Argentina's most popular type of Latin music, created in Cordoba

Safety and Scams

Argentina is one of the safest countries for travelers in Latin America, but petty crime does occur. Here's what to look out for to stay safe.

Petty crime is most common in and around public transport hubs in Buenos Aires and Mendoza. Recently, thieves have been targeting passports.

Be aware, criminals have been known to use force if they encounter resistance from travelers, so it's advisable to immediately hand over all cash and valuables when confronted or cornered.

Pickpockets

These opportunists are rife on public transport and around transport hubs. They are often neatly dressed and will often try to grab bags from between people's feet. Some will even come cruising past you on a skateboard or motorcycle, grab what they want and take off.

You can reduce the chance of being targeted if you avoid wearing expensive watches or jewelry, or carrying cameras that are tempting targets for thieves.

Electronic goods such as smartphones and iPads are expensive in Argentina, so they are highly prized goods for thieves. Avoid using them in public spaces or leaving them unsecured. Travelers have reported

Humahuaca carnival, Jujuy province

having their phones snatched from their hands while using them.

Only carry the cash you need for the day, avoid riding the subway late at night, and be careful when withdrawing cash from ATMs, as it's common for thefts to take place. Stay alert at all times and if possible only use ATMs in banks or hotels.

Taxi safety

When using taxis, if possible, book in advance. Only use radio taxis or a remise (a private car with driver).

Radio taxis have a clearly visible company logo on the rear passenger doors.

Taxis are a common place for counterfeiters to ply their trade. Unscrupulous taxi drivers, and sometimes street vendors, pretend to help travelers review their pesos, then trade fake bills for good ones.

Where to get help

The Argentine police operate a 24-hour police helpline in English for visitors in Buenos Aires, which can be accessed by dialing 101.

Another option is to contact the *Comisaria del Turista* (Tourist Police Station) at Av. Corrientes 436, or on the multi-lingual toll-free number 0800 999 5000 or by dialing directly on 4346 5748.

In Mendoza, you can seek assistance from the Tourist Police, San Martin 1143, by calling telephone 0261 4132135.

LGBTQ Travel in Argentina

Lesbian, gay, bisexual, transgender, and queer rights in Argentina are among the most advanced in the world.

Pride Parade

Argentina was the first country in Latin America, and the second in the Western Hemisphere after Canada, to implement marriage equality (in July 2010). Since 1983, when Argentina transitioned from a dictatorship to democracy, legal protections, inclusivity, and public acceptance of LGBTQ people and their rights have gained considerable ground. The right to change legal gender (without burdensome or humiliating paperwork and approvals) was put in place in 2012, the same year legislation was introduced fortifying legal protections based on sexual orientation, gender identity and expression.

Societal acceptance is remarkably high, with a 2013 Pew Center poll ranking Argentina the Latin American country with the most positive societal attitudes towards homosexuality. And let's not forget one-time first lady Eva Perón, an enduring gay icon both for her strength in the face of intolerance among the wealthy classes, and also for her support and protection of gay people at time when that was not at all common.

Gay Argentina

The capital and largest city, Buenos Aires, is home to a vibrant gay scene, which is spread out across this sprawling city, with concentrations of LGBTQ-oriented businesses in the residential Palermo neighborhood, as well as a handful of fun places in the tony Recoleta and hip San Telmo districts.

The early-bird watering hole is Pride Cafe in San Telmo, but the real party happens late night. Glam in Recoleta is a boys' favorite for electronic and latin pop, or catch a drag show at Sitges in Palermo. Nighttours (https://www.nighttours.com/buenosaires/) provides a good overview of gay Buenos Aires. BsAs is also home to Argentina's growing queer tango movement.

But Argentina is more than just its capital: LGBTQ visitors will find activities, events, bars, and restaurants in Cordoba, with its high concentration of university students; mountainous and picturesque Bariloche, especially during ski season; and Mendoza, the Napa Valley of Argentina, best known for its viniculture.

LGBTQ Festivals

Here are Argentina's top two LGBTQ events to keep in mind to make your visit extra special:

LGBTQ Pride Parade, Buenos Aires. Held annually in early November.

Gay Vendimia, Mendoza. The week-long festival held in early March, during the grape harvest, celebrating all things wine, and Argentina's second largest LGBTQ event (after Pride).

Visas & Vaccinations

A visit to Argentina might involve a hike through a subtropical jungle, or climbing the highest peak in the Americas (or both). Here's what you need to know before you go.

Citizens of the United States, Australia, Canada, and many European countries, among others, do not currently require a visa for travel to Argentina as long as their stay does not exceed 90 days, although payment of a reciprocity fee might be required from some nationalities before arrival.

Citizens of some other countries can enter Argentina without a visa for up to 30 or 60 days, while a number of nationalities will need to apply for a visa – the Argentina department of immigration is a good place to start (http://www.migraciones.gov.ar/accesible/indexN.php?visas). It's highly recommended that your passport is valid for at least six months after your date of entry.

Be aware that visa requirements are subject to frequent changes, so it's important to check the latest visa updates with your country's Embassy or Consulate for Argentina.

Vaccinations

Make sure you're up to date with all routine vaccinations before your trip to Argentina – the hepatitis A and typhoid vaccines are also highly recommended. Depending on your itinerary, length of stay, activities, and recent visits to other destinations, some travelers might also require additional vaccinations such as rabies and hepatitis B. Vaccination against yellow fever is strongly recommended if traveling to the regions bordering Paraguay and Brazil. If you've visited Misiones Province in the six days prior to your return home, many countries will ask you for a valid Yellow Fever Vaccination Certificate on re-entry.

Always ask your local travel clinic for advice regarding vaccinations.

Zika and other health concerns

The Zika virus is present in Argentina, and the risk of visiting the country should be evaluated by all travelers. Other mosquito-borne illnesses, such as Dengue fever, may also pose a risk, especially in the subtropical northeast. Using an effective insect repellent is recommended in areas where mosquitoes might be present.

Acute mountain sickness becomes a risk any time you climb above a certain altitude, and Argentina is home to some of the highest mountains outside of Asia. Some shortness of breath and fatigue is normal at high elevations, but seek medical help if you feel nauseated, experience severe headaches, or become disoriented.

Drink plenty of water, and avoid smoking and alcohol, both of which can worsen the effects. It's wise to spend a few days acclimatizing before heading out on a trek.

> "Acute mountain sickness becomes a risk any time you climb above a certain altitude, and Argentina is home to some of the highest mountains outside of Asia.

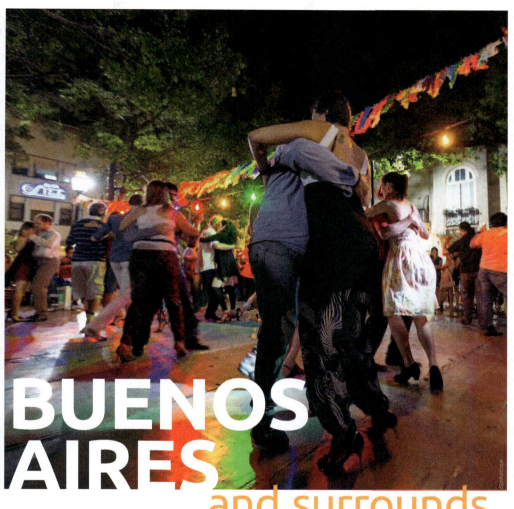

BUENOS AIRES
and surrounds

O ften called the "Paris of South America" due to its large number of French-style buildings, Buenos Aires is busy, diverse, and very cosmopolitan – but also friendly and relaxed, with an enormous variety of things to see and do.

BUENOS AIRES & SURROUNDS

Local's guide to Buenos Aires

If there's anything Buenos Aires has to spare, it's character. Emblematic spots like San Telmo (famous for tango) and La Boca (known for its colorful buildings) are just the beginning – behind all 48 Porteñian neighborhoods lies the passion and tradition of its people.

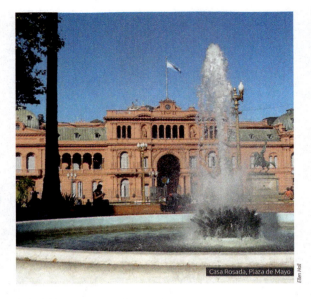
Casa Rosada, Plaza de Mayo

Getting around

Most of the attractions are geographically located in the western strip of the city, which faces the Rio de la Plata and is where it all started: the Port. That's why locals are called *porteños*.

The public transport network will take you anywhere you want to go in the city. There are seven metro lines, countless buses, and intercity trains. Prepaid SUBE Cards, available in authorized Tourist Centres and subway stations, can be used for all public transit and topped up at kiosks around the city.

Taxis can get expensive, and traffic is mayhem – but taxis are the safest way to get around at night. You can hail one (look for the lit "Libre" sign in the windshield), but it's best to call a Radio taxi or UBER.

Historic Monserrat

The Monserrat district is Buenos Aires' historic heart, filled with government buildings and French-style architecture. Plaza de Mayo is the main square of the city, where most political life takes place.

Puerto Madero, Retiro, and Recoleta

A few minutes' walk from Plaza de Mayo is the Obelisk, Buenos Aires' most iconic monument. Cross the famously

Recoleta Cemetery

> **You'll end up in Recoleta, famous for its cemetery, where you can visit the graves of Eva Perón and other important figures.**

BUENOS AIRES & SURROUNDS

Political street art about the "disappeared" in La Boca

wide 9 de Julio Avenue and head to Puerto Madero, a modern, stylish district and a great sunset spot: grab a drink and enjoy the views of the river.

Or go north along Florida Street, with its elegant Galerías Pacífico mall, and through Retiro; you'll end up in Recoleta, famous for its cemetery, where you can visit the graves of Eva Perón and other important figures. Go on Sunday when nearby Plaza Francia bustles with musicians and an artisans' market.

Palermo and Belgrano

Palermo is subdivided into several districts: the Soho, Palermo Chico, Palermo Viejo, Palermo Hollywood, and Las Cañitas. It's best explored on foot, so wear comfy shoes.

The Bosques of Palermo is Buenos Aires' main park, with lakes, a planetarium, and a rose garden. Also worthwhile: the Japanese Gardens, artsy stores in the Soho, and horse races at Palermo Hipódromo.

The up-and-coming subdistrict of Las Cañitas is a local favorite. Elegant, trendy, and compact, Cañitas is full of restaurants, shops, and charming boulevards.

In Belgrano, you'll find Chinatown, packed with markets, spices, and quirky gift shops. Museo Larreta houses a hidden gem: the Spanish-style Andaluz Garden. Enjoy an afternoon concert or do a nighttime guided tour.

Traditional districts

Don't miss the local Friday night ritual: go to one of Corrientes Avenue's theatres – the blocks between Florida and Callao have options for any budget – followed by dinner in a classic pizzeria like Los Inmortales, Guerrín, or El Cuartito.

> **The Bosques of Palermo is Buenos Aires' main park, with lakes, a planetarium, and a rose garden.**

BUENOS AIRES & SURROUNDS

Julio's, aka "the Craa" Salon in Villa Crespo

Visiting one of the *cafetines* – small, classic cafés – is also a must. The most famous is the Tortoni, but El Gato Negro is arguably more interesting, with a wide variety of cafés, chocolates, and teas you can purchase by weight.

Towards the geographic center of the city is Almagro, a very traditional district usually overlooked by visitors. Be sure to try El Molino Dorado – only open for dinner, this tiny Russian restaurant is a well-kept secret.

Between Almagro and Palermo Soho is the culturally diverse Villa Crespo district. For an experience to brag about back home, get a haircut at Julio Pan's salon, aka "the Craa." Julio is the barber to Argentina's football stars. He opens after 6pm every night, and just going to see his place is worth it.

For shopping, Serrano and Malabia Streets between Corrientes and Córdoba is the fashion outlet area and one of the funkiest parts of town. Go for *merienda* (afternoon tea) at Malvón – you'll thank us.

Markets and museums

Some of the best insider gems tucked away in the city are the markets. Check out Mercado el Progreso in Caballito, focused on gastronomy, and Mercado de Pulgas, in Chacarita, selling antiques, arts, and handicrafts.

The arts scene is quite intense in Buenos Aires. Beyond the famous MALBA and la Usina del Arte, there's Centro Cultural Kirchner, a huge exhibition hub just a few blocks from Puerto Madero.

If you're into architecture, the Colón Theatre is an absolute must, rivaling La Scala opera house in Milan. Guided tours are available in English and Spanish.

If you enjoy dancing and drums, head to the Centro Cultural Konex, in Almagro, on a Monday evening and dance to the rhythm of La Bomba del Tiempo.

> **If you're into architecture, the Colón Theatre is an absolute must, rivaling La Scala opera house in Milan.**

Teatro Colón

BUENOS AIRES & SURROUNDS

Nightlife

BsAs is a 24/7 oasis of cool – but at night, the party doesn't really get started until well after 2am.

Bars

Start your night at one of the laid-back bars in the city's oldest neighborhood, San Telmo. Doppelganger (locally called Doppel) specializes in classic cocktails like negronis. Napoles Bar was once a massive storage unit for an antiques collector – he decided to put his wares on display and added a well-stocked bar for good measure.

Speakeasies

Buenos Aires has a lively underground bar scene. Speakeasies with hidden doors are everywhere – such as Florería Atlántico in Recoleta, a chic cocktail bar masquerading as flower shop.

In Palermo, try the Verne Club for its author-inspired menu and absinthe tasting before lining up for the city's newest hot spot, Uptown, a full-on homage to the New York subway.

Located on a quiet street in Villa Crespo, 878 may seem out of the way, but it's easily the most welcoming underground bar in the city.

Clubs

Niceto Vega in Palermo is Buenos Aires' street of nightclubs. Head to Club 69 at the Niceto Club to see and be seen – if the music is all that matters, hit up the Under Club for house and techno, or try Makena Cantina Club for live music.

Milongas

An Argentina night without tango would be a sin. Maldita is a classic *milonga* (tango house) and its live orchestra, El Atronfe, draws a crowd. For newbies, your best bet is the informal La Cathedral. For serious night owls, La Virtua even serves patrons breakfast after 4am to keep them dancing.

I came to Buenos Aires for four months to immerse myself in tango. After two years of taking classes, and devouring the moves of my favorite *tangueras* on YouTube, I was hungry to live it. My plan was to take lessons every day from a variety of *maestros*, and to dance at a different *milonga* every night. I timed my trip to coincide with three back-to-back tango festivals: The International Tango Festival and World Cup, *Milongueando*, and *Mujercitas*. At the workshops, I met people from many countries who all had the same crazy idea: to live and breathe tango as intensely as possible. Their camaraderie was as vital to my progress as all the formal instruction I received.

Julia Melancon, Writer and Traveler

BUENOS AIRES & SURROUNDS

Day Trips from Buenos Aires

From picturesque towns to traditional folk fairs, there are a number of scenic day trips less than an hour from Buenos Aires.

Colonia del Sacramento

Colonia del Sacramento

A 50-minute ferry ride across the Rio de la Plata from Buenos Aires, this cobblestoned gem is one of the oldest towns in Uruguay. Be sure to check out the Historic Quarter (a UNESCO World-Heritage site), Street of Sighs (La Calle de los Suspiros), Faro Lighthouse, Puerta de la Ciudadela (drawbridge), and Paseo de San Gabriel, where you can watch the sun set over the river. Ferry tickets can be purchased online via Buquebus, (US $80-250/$2,095-6,550 ARS round trip). Buquebus' online platform can be tricky to navigate, but it's advisable to reserve in advance. Ferries leave three times a day from Puerto Madero.

Feria de Mataderos

This popular outdoor street fair, located on the outskirts of the city in the Mataderos neighborhood, is an hour by a public bus from central Buenos Aires. The fair takes place every Sunday (approximately March-December). Visitors can explore gaucho culture, enjoy folk music and dance performances, taste traditional food, watch a local game of *pato* (a sport combining elements of polo and basketball), and shop for artisanal crafts. Or pop into the Museo de Criollo de los Corrales, a small museum showcasing Argentine cowboy life (US $1.40/$37 ARS). Entrance to the fair is free, but call ahead to confirm that it's open.

Tigre

Ask a *porteño* to suggest a day trip, and chances are they'll recommend Tigre, a small river town on the Parana Delta 20mi (32km) outside of Buenos Aires. You can get here in about an hour on the Mitre train which runs every 10 minutes from the Retiro Station for US $0.50 ($13 ARS) round trip. Tigre's main attraction is a boat tour through the Parana Delta, where you can soak up the lush countryside while learning the history of the area. These tours can be hired leaving from Puerto Madero in Buenos Aires or, more casually and on the spot, from Tigre's river port. Afterwards, explore the ornate Museo de Arte Tigre, once a luxury hotel (US $2.50/$66 ARS). Don't miss the Puerto de Frutos Market, 20 minutes by foot from Tigre's train station, to shop for local crafts, treats, and antiques.

> **This cobblestoned gem is one of the oldest towns in Uruguay.**

THE NORTH

Northern Argentina stands out for its distinctive landscapes – sub-tropical rainforest and mighty waterfalls in the Northeast, surreal salt flats and multi-colored hills in the Northwest – and its ancient cultural roots.

THE NORTH

Northeast Argentina

Along the Uruguay and Parana rivers lies the Littoral. With landscapes that vary from the extreme stillness of the wetlands to the most powerful waterfall system on earth, the Northeast belongs to peace seekers and intrepid adventurers.

Gualeguaychu carnival

It's worth devoting two weeks to exploring the "Argentine Mesopotamia" and falling into its slow rhythm. Though generally less expensive than Buenos Aires and Patagonia, you may need to rent a vehicle to get to some hidden gems.

This region is culturally rich, as indigenous tribes still live here. Make a point of visiting their communities and learning about their history and traditions.

If it takes you months to remove the red soil from your clothes, then you can say you've truly seen the region!

Rosario

The "cradle of the flag" is a four-hour drive from Buenos Aires, and the typical starting point for an itinerary across the Littoral. Considered one of the country's main cultural hubs, many Argentinian icons were born here – Che Guevara, Lionel Messi, even Argentina's flag.

Though Rosario is usually overlooked during short itineraries, it's well worth a visit for its vibrant arts scene – check out the Silos Davis museum – and a riverfront lined with parks and pubs. If you visit during spring/summer, catch the 15-min ferry from La Fluvial to "La Isla," and enjoy a day at one of the many beach bars overlooking the city. Or hire a kayak to explore areas of the delta that not many people have access to.

Among rivers in Entre Ríos

Entre Ríos hosts Argentina's most important festival: the Gualeguaychú Carnival, celebrated during January and February.

But Entre Ríos is more than colored feathers and bling – it also offers a wide range of outdoor activities and a well-developed tourism industry. Try your hand at La Paz, the best fishing spot in Entre Ríos. Or visit the Termas de Colón, one of many thermal baths in the province.

It's fairly easy to get around using the long-distance buses network: Flechabus is the main operator in the region. Campsites, hostels, and ecotourism resorts are numerous and affordable.

> " Considered one of the country's main cultural hubs, many Argentinian icons were born here – Che Guevara, Lionel Messi, even Argentina's flag.

THE NORTH

If you come around Carnival time, you'll need to book in advance and be prepared for high temperatures and humidity.

Corrientes: Sport Fishing and Esteros del Ibera

Travelers come to Corrientes province for two main reasons: the Esteros del Ibera, and world-class recreational fishing.

The Esteros del Ibera is the second-most important wetland in the continent. Though not yet an official national park, it's gaining fame due to its huge variety of flora and fauna, including caiman, capybara, and over 360 species of birds. Visit now, while it's still off the main tourism radar.

The Esteros can be accessed several ways. There are some eco-lodges near the northernmost point, but most visitors arrive via the town of Mercedes, about 68mi (110 km) south of the Esteros, where you can rent a car or take a bus to Colonia Carlos Pellegrini, a small village just outside park. You'll find numerous accommodation options here, including eco-lodges and campsites.

It's highly recommended to rent a car (ideally an SUV) as there's not a wide range of public transport. Or, you can arrange a guided visit from Colonia Carlos Pellegrini or Mercedes, or book an all-inclusive package to stay within the park for around three days.

If you're interested in recreational fishing, head to Goya or Paso de la Patria, famed hubs for Dorado and Surubí fish. You can organize your own adventure or hire a guide.

Iguazu Falls

Misiones beyond Iguazu Falls

Magnificent Iguazu Falls is the main draw to this region, and with good reason. But if you take time to venture further, you'll be well rewarded.

Renting a car is recommended if you want explore the region in depth.

If you're arriving from Corrientes, and want to visit the UNESCO-listed Ruinas de San Ignacio (a Jesuit Mission founded in 1632), consider overnighting at Saltos del Tabay, a huge campsite 29mi (46km) away, near the Parana River.

From here, the Saltos del Mocona is worth a detour – this unique waterfall runs parallel to its river for 1.8mi (3km). The falls are visible for about 250 days per year when the river's not at peak fullness. Before going, check the official website as the park closes on occasion due to weather conditions. If you don't have a car, head to El Soberbio; there, you'll find the only official transport that operates in the area.

Other popular waterfalls can be found in the vicinity of Puerto Iguazu: Salto de Mbocay and Salto del Turista.

> **Magnificent Iguazu Falls is the main draw to this region, and with good reason. But if you take time to venture further, you'll be well rewarded.**

THE NORTH

The Northwest

When we talk about Argentina, we talk about diversity and the strong influence of European immigration all over the country. But if we're looking for a region that still keeps its native roots alive, that's el Norte.

Catamarca Province

A journey to the North starts in Catamarca, where the thermal baths of Fiambalá have become both a travel and a health destination for people looking to relieve pain or stress. A short distance away is Antofagasta de la Sierra, an expanse of rocks and desert until you reach a few huge lakes filled with crystal water and hundreds of flamingos.

Tucuman Province

In the arid North, the lush hill town of Tafi del Valle feels like an oasis, surrounded by rolling green mountains and fields. The city center is lined with little shops selling artisan products,

Lake with flamingos, Catamarca

including local cheese and wool sweaters. Another worthwhile stop on the road towards Salta is the Ruinas de Quilmes, a fortified citadel built around 850 AD by the pre-Columbian Quilmes people.

Salta Province

Once in Salta, the mountains of the Calchaqui Valley take on hues of red and gold. Your first stop should be the village of La Poma, home to El Puente del Diablo: caves formed by the erosion of volcanic stones that display stunning colors thanks to the minerals in the earth. You'll find small geysers and beautiful formations of stalagmites and stalactites.

The area is also famous for the UNESCO-listed Graneros Incaicos, 24 roofed structures of mud and straw, built 900 years ago by the Inca to store grain and ears of corn. They're held

Salta cathedral

> **You reach a few huge lakes filled with crystal water and hundreds of flamingos.**

THE NORTH

inside a huge natural cavern 115ft (35m) long. Inside, you'll see measurements carved in stone, and cave paintings thought to be instructions on how to use the granaries: when a group passed through, they left the silos full of grain for the next group that arrived.

Not far from La Poma is Cachi, a handsome little town built of white adobe buildings in the classic northern style. Cachi is surrounded by organic plantations of red pepper, the main local crop. The peppers are used to produce high-quality paprika, as its flavor is quite intense.

Salta is the main city of the province, known for its ornate colonial buildings, lively *peñas* (folklore concerts), and excellent regional cuisine. It's well worth a day or two of exploration.

Your last destination before heading to Jujuy is the mountain town of Iruya. Here, at the "Mirador del Condor," you might get a glimpse of the majestic Andean condor, one of the largest birds in the world.

Jujuy Province

Visit the spectacular Quebrada de Humahuaca, a UNESCO-listed valley that undulates in colorful waves along the Rio Grande; the lovely village of Purmamarca, just below the famous "Hill of Seven Colors;" and Pucara de Tilcara, a strategically located pre-Inca fortification.

Stop for a glass of *api* (a purple, corn-based drink), some *humitas* (savory corn cakes), or tamales made with *charqui* (dried meat), followed by *anchi*, a dessert made with cornmeal. And

Iruya village

don't forget to try the various types of potatoes from the Humahuaca valley.

Almost to the border of Bolivia is the Cerro Huancar, a high mountain covered with sand dunes. Huancar is popular with sand-boarding fans but best known for its lively Carnival (February-March). If you drive here during the celebration, you'll often see groups of people on the side of the road dancing, drinking, and wearing a "devil" disguise – the party can continue for up to a month.

Though people from the Northwest are largely Catholic (and particularly devoted to the Virgin Mary), they also maintain many of their aboriginal beliefs. For example, on August 1 it's customary to say "thank you" to Mother Earth, and ask for blessings by making a hole on the ground and dropping in beer, wine, cigarettes, and food to "feed" the Pachamama. During Day of the Dead (October 31- November 2), it's common to see women cooking pastries. The belief is that while the soul is in purgatory, it gets hungry and thirsty, so cooking and praying for the departed can help them on their long journey.

> **"**
> **Your last destination before heading to Jujuy is the mountain town of Iruya. Here, at the "Mirador del Condor," you might get a glimpse of the majestic Andean condor.**

CENTRAL ARGENTINA

Rolling foothills and quaint alpine villages, high-elevation vineyards backed by snowy peaks, epic white-water rafting and lunar landscapes – the heart of the country offers plenty of variety.

CENTRAL ARGENTINA

The Central Sierras

The Sierras Centrales aren't on most travelers' lists of places to visit in Argentina – but locals have long been aware of the region's astonishing landscapes, cultural experiences, and warm hospitality.

Explore Cordoba and Los Gigantes

Cordoba, Argentina's second-oldest city, is known for its universities, relaxed atmosphere, and well-preserved colonial architecture. But adventure seekers should head to Los Gigantes, on the Camino de las Altas Cumbres – these are towering, vertical rock formations with small green valleys in between.

The most impressive is the Valle de Los Lisos, with 11 trekking circuits organized into some 40 paths classified by difficulty. These will lead you to caves, waterfalls, underground rivers, and streams enclosed by huge, rocky walls.

The reserve is private and there's a fee for use of the circuits. If you stay the night, there are several mountain shelters that must be booked in advance, or you can camp. All-inclusive tours are also available, with guides, meals, and accommodation packages for one to three days. Prices start from US $60 ($1,580 ARS).

Relax in Valle de Traslasierra

The peaceful village of Nono has the

Los Gigantes, Cordoba

perfect anti-stress formula. Beside the pristine Chico River, you'll find extensive golden beaches gleaming with mica, and banks lined with huge, rounded rocks that form natural pools and small waterfalls. Let yourself be enveloped by the sound of the water, the song of the birds, and the smell of the herbs that grow here, and enjoy being in the middle of an authentic natural spa.

If you prefer a bit of adrenaline, you can kayak, ride horses, or rappel in the area. Or you can climb neighboring Mount Champaqui, the highest peak in Cordoba Province.

Find adventure (and maybe aliens)

Some areas of this region are considered energetic centers, due to the high quantity of quartz in the terrain. Uritorco Mount is one of them. A favorite of backpackers and campers,

> **The reserve is private and there's a fee for use of the circuits. If you stay the night, there are several mountain shelters that must be booked in advance, or you can camp.**

CENTRAL ARGENTINA

this mount is a center for legends and mysticism, including some alien theories – you might consider it the Roswell of Argentina. Some people believe extraterrestrials called Erks live in an ethereal city under the mount. It's fairly easy to climb, and if you spend the night there, you'll see some lights in the sky that scientists can't explain.

A 25-min drive from Capilla del Monte, you'll find one of the region's loveliest trekking circuits, Los Terrones. The moderate trails run through an incredible landscape of red rock formations that form mysterious shapes.

Not far away is San Marcos Sierras, a little hippie town where a community of people live off the grid. The main mount here is Alpha Mount, ideal for viewing the sunset. Follow the path along the Quilpo River and immerse yourself in one of the purest areas of the province, where you can actually hear the silence.

Discover a slice of Europe

La Cumbrecita, one of the most beautiful villages in the province, is a little Tyrolean hamlet with authentic German-style architecture and cuisine. Set in the middle of the mountains, the town is entirely pedestrian. From the center of town, several paths will take you to small falls, streams, and natural pools. Don't forget to try one of the local artisan beers.

For a different flavor, La Cumbre, Cruz Chica and Los Cocos are three charming villages with a British influence. Several grand English manor houses have been converted in hotels if you want to relax in style. Try to find

Alta Gracia

your way out of the grass labyrinth in Los Cocos, or take the chairlift up the mountain, and zipline or alpine-slide your way down. Or visit the Road of the Artisans, which links the villages of La Cumbre and Villa Giardina, to buy some local handicrafts.

Visit the home of a legend

In Cordoba province, you'll find many vestiges of Spanish colonialism, as well as a strong Jesuit legacy. Many of the buildings are still standing, and some have been declared UNESCO World-Heritage sites. One of the most important is the 17th-century Jesuit estancia in Alta Gracia. This village is also known as the childhood home of Che Guevara. Today, his home is a small museum, where you can see his room, his bed, and some of his personal objects.

When to go

If you want to skip the crowds, avoid going to Cordoba during the summer (January and February), winter break (July), and national holidays. The best seasons? Spring and autumn: good weather, fewer crowds, and best prices.

> **Alta Gracia is also known as the childhood home of Che Guevara.**

CENTRAL ARGENTINA

The Midwest: Mendoza and Beyond

There's more to El Cuyo than Mendoza — and there's more to Mendoza than wine. From South America's tallest mountain to otherworldly landscapes and soothing hot springs, discover the secrets of the Argentine midwest.

Mendoza vineyards with Aconcagua in the background

Mendoza

If you're going to Mendoza, there will of course be wine. But if you only hit one wine trail, make sure it's the Uco Valley. Situated along the Tunuyán River, this prominent wine-growing region is famous for Malbec, but it's the unpretentious vibe mixed with the breathtaking backdrop of the Cordón de Plata mountains that makes this valley special.

When you're done grape-sampling, do as the locals do and head out to Lake Potrerillos on a summer weekend for sunbathing, swimming, and relaxing surrounded by snow-capped peaks and cypress forests.

Just north is the quaint little town of Uspallata, your jumping-off point to explore the Inca petroglyphs at Cerro Tunduqueral (where some of *Seven Years in Tibet* was filmed). Check out Los Paramillos, a petrified forest often called the Bosque de Darwin as a nod to its discoverer.

Stop at the Puente del Inca, a natural arch over the Rio Vacas, on your way to Aconcagua, South America's tallest mountain. A day hike to the first base camp, Confluencia, is worth it for the incredible views. Alternately, head south to see Volcano Tupungato, one of the tallest volcanoes in the world.

If you're in Mendoza in early March, you're in luck. The *Fiesta de la Vendimia*, or Annual Grape Harvest Festival, is a 10-day affair celebrated across the region. You'll witness folk dancing, massive parades, endless wine tastings, and a pageant where beauty queens from Mendoza's 18 districts compete to be crowned the Harvest Queen.

Malargue

South of Mendoza proper is Malargue, where you'll find La Laguna de la Niña Encantada, a lovely lake with crystal-clear, turquoise waters. Drive on to Valle de Las Leñas, a popular ski resort in winter turned natural paradise in the summer. Hike, mountain bike, or horseback through the aptly named

> " The *Fiesta de la Vendimia*, or Annual Grape Harvest Festival, is a 10-day affair celebrated across the region.

CENTRAL ARGENTINA

Valle Hermoso before heading off to relax at El Azufres hot springs.

South of Malargue is the *Caverna de las Brujas*, or Witches Cave, a nature reserve that's home to one of the largest cave complexes in Argentina. Nearby is Cascadas de Manqui Malal, 98ft (30m) waterfalls covered in fossilized remains. The area is perfect for hiking, climbing, or mountain biking – and there's a campsite if you want to stay the night.

Next, head to the high-altitude Laguna Llancanelo, known for its flamingos. While water birds are the main attraction, it's worth checking out *la Cueva del Tigre* (the Cave of the Tiger) and the Laguna de Carilauquen while on site.

Continue south to the Reserva la Provincial la Payunia, a relatively inaccessible but staggeringly beautiful reserve boasting more than 800 volcanoes – one of the highest concentrations of volcanoes on the planet. Sometimes referred to as the Patagonia of Mendoza, La Payunia is also an amazing place to spot wildlife – such as condors, pumas, eagles, foxes, and even guanacos (a llama relative) – or even the odd cave painting or two.

La Rioja and San Juan

La Rioja and San Juan are best known for their two star attractions: Ischigualasto, aka the *Valle de la Luna* (Valley of the Moon), famed for its bizarre rock formations and some of the earliest known dinosaur remains; and Talampaya National Park, with its 656ft

Ischigualasto

(200m) high red sandstone cliffs, Triassic-period fossils, and 1,500-year-old rock carvings.

To visit the parks, stay in Villa Unión in La Rioja or the quaint town of San Agustín de Valle Fértil in San Juan. Talampaya especially merits a longer stay – be sure to start early, when the morning sun hits the colored rocks and illuminates the canyon.

Afterwards, explore the Laguna Brava Provincial Reserve, which boasts stunning colors and ample wildlife, before heading to Valle de Calingasta. Star-gazers must stop in Barreal to visit the Complejo Astronómico El Leoncito, one of the continent's most important space observatories, inside of El Leoncito National Park.

Finally, head west to Las Hornillas, the point of departure for adventurous treks and climbs at Cerro Mercedario, a favorite summit amongst mountaineers and the eighth-highest mountain of the Andes, before trekking back to Mendoza for a farewell glass of Malbec.

> **Explore the Laguna Brava Provincial Reserve, which boasts stunning colors and ample wildlife.**

PATAGONIA

For lovers of nature, Patagonia's siren call is irresistible. Its wonders are as many as the region is vast, starting with the crystal-blue waters of Lake Nahuel Huapi, the pinnacles and ice fields of Los Glaciares National Park, and the rocky Atlantic beaches where penguins nest by the thousands.

PATAGONIA

The Lake District

With alpine lakes ranging from milky green to eye-popping azure and a backdrop of snow-dusted mountains, Argentina's Lake District is prime for exploration.

Discover hidden beaches filled with mauve and teal stones along Nahuel Huapi, the largest lake in the region. On misty mornings, keep your eyes peeled for the lake monster Nahuelito.

Parque Nacional Nahuel Huapi

South America's oldest national park can be divided into north and south. The northern section includes the famous Route of the Seven Lakes, connecting the towns of San Martin de los Andes and Villa La Angostura.

Villa Traful

About 16mi (25km) off Ruta 40 from Confluencia is Villa Traful, with lakeshore campgrounds filled with rowdy backpackers in the summer. Lago Traful is magical and well worth a day trip from one of the larger towns (pack a picnic lunch).

Bariloche

On the southeast shores of Lago Nahuel Huapi, San Carlos de Bariloche is the gateway city to the southern section of the park and offers year-round activities. Visitors can also arrive from Chile by a scenic lake crossing through the Andes via Puerto Blest,

View from Cerro Campanario

the same route taken by Patagonian explorers (US $280 /$6,825 ARS).

Unless you've come especially for winter sports, consider visiting in spring or fall for low-season prices and more solitary hikes. In March and April, the hillsides turn into a rainbow of orange and magenta *lengas*. November brings fierce Patagonian winds and blooms of golden scotch broom alongside indigo lupines and wild orchids. Rainy days can be spent tasting exquisite local chocolate.

Circuito Chico

Don't miss the view – considered one of the world's most stunning – from Cerro Campanario, located 20 minutes from downtown Bariloche along a public bus route. You can reach the top in less than an hour; non-hikers can take the chairlift to the top. Try the lemon pie and *cafe con leche* at the *confiteria*.

> "
> **Don't miss the view – considered one of the world's most stunning – from Cerro Campanario.**

PATAGONIA

Short Hikes
The Llao Llao Municipal Park in Circuito Chico has many interconnecting trails. Cerrito Llao Llao is a gentle one-hour climb with a stunning view of Brazo Blest, Cerro Capilla, and the Chilean Andes.

For a singular view of Brazo Tristeza, try the Bahia Lopez trail, also under an hour to the lookout.

Or, starting about a mile past the Llao Llao hotel, a 20-minute walk in the forest will take you to a tiny clearing with native arrayan trees. Continue along this trail to secluded, wind-protected beaches on Lago Moreno.

Beaches
Bahia de Los Troncos and Villa Tacul are best on days without wind; otherwise head to the sheltered eastern side of Playa Morenito (near Bahía Pascasio, with excellent local beer and kayak rentals).

Colonia Suiza
This quaint three-block settlement is nestled on the shore of Lake Moreno, just a 30-minute bus from downtown Bariloche. Along with a public beach and campgrounds, the village also boasts several restaurants serving *curanto*, an *asado* dug into the ground. For *curanto*, visit on Wednesday or Sunday; there's also a small local craft fair on weekends.

Overnight Hikes
Once the snow melts, you'll be overwhelmed by the hiking possibilities; check with the Club Andino to see which trails and accommodation are open. January-April are the best months. If you didn't bring gear, you can always splurge with a night at a *refugio* (US $25/$655 ARS). If you've got room in your pack, bring along a bottle of wine to share over dinner – you'll make lots of friends later when someone breaks out a guitar. Things can get festive at the *refugios*, so if you're looking for quiet, camp outside and pay a small fee to use the kitchen.

For an up-to-four-night trek without a guide, start at the base of Cerro Catedral and hike up to Frey, Jacob, Laguna Negra, and Lopez *refugios*, spending a night at each. The trek can be done in reverse order, or any combination of one- two- or three-day hikes as well.

Tronador and Mascardi
Parque Nacional Nahuel Huapi extends

> **If you've got room in your pack, bring along a bottle of wine to share over dinner – you'll make lots of friends later when someone breaks out a guitar.**

Hiking the Lake District

PATAGONIA

A refugio

as far south as the Lago Mascardi recreational area with access to Mount Tronador, an extinct stratovolcano providing some of the best trekking in the region. The three-day trek Pampa Linda-Meiling-Rocca via Glacier Alerce is spectacular if you can swing it (US $200/$5,240 ARS for guided crossing, gear included).

Non-campers can spend the night at Hotel Tronador or Hosteria Pampa Linda. For day access, buses leave from the Club Andino at 8:30am and return 5:30pm (two hours from Bariloche). If you're in your own vehicle, check for entry/exit times.

Kawén Adventures provides exceptional half- and full-day kayaking tours on Lago Mascardi.

If you're headed south to the hippie town of El Bolson, veer off Ruta 40 to visit Lago Steffen, the warmest lake in the area for swimmers.

Parque Nacional Lanin

The only national park in Argentina to be jointly run by the government and local indigenous communities, Parque Nacional Lanin is unique for its prehistoric-looking monkey-puzzle trees.

The Lanin volcano, towering over Lago Huechulafquen at 12,000ft (3,658m), is the only active volcano in the Argentina Lake District. Trained hikers can summit Lanin: a three-day hike on the glacier, ice-walking gear and registration required. Excursions leave from sleepy Junin de los Andes, the closest town, with a border crossing to Pucon, Chile (around four hours by car).

You'll need a car to explore the Park, as there is no public transport. There are several campgrounds on the northern coast of Huechulafquen, many offering simple meals and hot water; the southern coast is rugged and although camping is permitted, there are no services.

Dinosaurs Are Big Here

The region around Neuquen, in the northern Lake District, boasts some of the richest paleontology sites in the world – *Giganotosaurus Carolinii* (one of the largest carnivores in the world, bigger than T-Rex) was found here in 1993. Here's where to get your fossil fix.

Villa el Chocon
Bachmann Museum hosts the original fossils of *Giganotosaurus*, found nearby, and its skeleton is almost 70% complete. The local tradition is to give the dinos a "surname" after their discoverer – in this case, Mr. Rubén Carolini. Ask the staff how to access the massive, foot-shaped "ponds" near the lake.

Plaza Huincul and Rincon de los Sauces
Carmen Funes Museum in Plaza has a full reconstruction of a *Argentinosaurus Huinculensis* skeleton (one of the largest known herbivores), along with a nest and eggs!

Lago los Barreales
Run by National University of Comahue, the Geology and Paleontology Museum allows visitors to witness life at a dinosaur excavation site. Reach out to the Centre before dropping by for the educational experience in the field.

Tips: This area is vast, so you'll need to get around by car. From Neuquén city, sites are about a one to three-hour drive. The museums are generally adapted houses/warehouses – don't expect American Museum of Natural History standards.

PATAGONIA

Southwest Patagonia

The words "Argentine Patagonia" typically conjure up images of the knife-edge peaks of Mount Fitz Roy, or colossal shards of ice calving off the Perito Moreno glacier. These places are famous for good reason — but beyond the heavy hitters, Patagonia offers a wealth of lesser-known alternatives with fewer visitors.

Fall colors at Mont Fitz Roy

The other side to El Perito Moreno

Astonishing in size and truly spectacular in form, El Perito Moreno — aka Argentina's most famous glacier — truly deserves to be called "unmissable." But a trip to the park can feel like your hard-earned pesos are disappearing more quickly than Patagonia's glaciers.

It's possible to visit on the cheap, although be aware that cheap is still a relative term. Hop on a public bus from the terminal (US $30/$786 ARS return) and pay your US $25 ($655 ARS) entrance fee to access the boardwalks that offer various perspectives of this ice giant's 3mi (5km) wide snout.

To get up close and personal, consider an afternoon of ice trekking, where you strap on your crampons to crunch across the surface of the ice, climbing through crevasses and shafts and getting to see what a glacier looks like. Expect to spend around US $130 ($3,405 ARS) for an hour and a half of activity.

Lesser-known trails in Los Glaciares National Park

78mi (125km) north of Perito Moreno lies Argentina's self-proclaimed hiking capital, El Chalten, which makes an excellent base for exploring the hiking trails of the northern sector of Los Glaciares National Park.

The most popular is the eight-hour round trip to Laguna de los Tres, an aquamarine glacial lake offering the ultimate views of Mount Fitz Roy. Although the hike is possible in one day, savvy trekkers pitch up at the free Poincenot campsite just before the final ascent to the lake, and head up for sunrise. You'll find fewer other hikers at this time and, if the weather's good, witness the spectacular moment when the granite peaks appear out of the early morning light.

But Los Glaciares National Park is packed with other trails beyond this crowd-pleaser. A detour on the return trip from Laguna de los Tres via

> **To get up close and personal, consider an afternoon of ice trekking, where you strap on your crampons to crunch across the surface of the ice.**

PATAGONIA

Perito Moreno

Laguna Madre and Laguna Hijo adds an extra 30 minutes to your descent, but promises spectacular lake vistas along a trail practically empty of hikers.

For a more challenging trek, the four-day Huemul Circuit – which requires experience and technical equipment, the latter of which you can rent in El Chalten – is quickly establishing itself as a unique alternative to the more famous W trek in Chile's Torres del Paine National Park.

Patagonia's most intrepid border crossing

If that doesn't satisfy your urge to get off the beaten trail, this trek over to Chile might just do it. The two-day, one-night adventure combines hiking and a boat journey as you cross from El Chalten in Argentina to Villa O'Higgins at the very end of the Carretera Austral in Chile – with stunning views of Fitz Roy, glaciers, and lakes to boot.

It's not a trip to be taken lightly – quite literally, as you'll be carrying all of your gear at least 9mi (15km) before reaching the boat to cross Lago O'Higgins – but it's well worth the effort. It's easy to feel like a pioneer as you pass through one of Patagonia's most unexplored reaches, and you might even catch a glimpse of the critically endangered huemul deer.

The other Perito Moreno

Heading north of El Chalten, the next 390mi (625km) of pampa is fairly sparse when it comes to tourist attractions, until you reach the Cueva de los Manos Pintados. Located near Perito Moreno – the town, not the glacier – this cave has the most impressive ancient paintings you'll find in Patagonia.

Dated at a whopping 7,300 years BC, the multi-colored, stencilled outlines of handprints are believed to show evidence of one of the earliest hunter-gatherer cultures in the continent – and look like they were painted just yesterday. Get here on a tour from nearby Perito Moreno or Los Antiguos and admire the handprints in all their splendor (look out for the one with six fingers), as well as the pictures of guanaco being hunted and shamanic ceremonies, all left for eternity on the rock face.

> " The four-day Huemel Circuit is quickly establishing itself as a unique alternative to the more famous W trek in Chile's Torre del Paine National Park.

PATAGONIA

Coastal Patagonia

Coastal Argentine Patagonia tends to be overshadowed by its more famous cousins El Chalten and El Calafate further south. But this region teems with wildlife – both prehistoric and very much alive – and is also home to the largest population of Welsh descendants in South America.

Killer whales in Peninsula Valdes

Ever seen an orca, aka a killer whale? Ever seen one hunt? If there's one place to rectify this, it's at Peninsula Valdes, a headland accessible from nearby Puerto Madryn and home to shallow bays, pebble beaches, and colonies of elephant seals and southern sea lions.

It's the latter that draw the orcas in droves – they've adopted a unique hunting strategy to prey on the animals at high tide, appearing to beach themselves as a ruse to catch unsuspecting young.

The technique is best observed at dawn from February to April at Punta Norte, a 2.5 hours' drive from Puerto Madryn. Tours are expensive (expect to pay over US $120/$3,145 ARS) but it's easy enough – and considerably cheaper – to rent a car for the day, giving you far more flexibility to check out the various marine wildlife around the peninsula.

The waters here are also home to

Whale watching, Peninsula Valdes

an important population of southern right whales, who spend the months of June to December breeding and raising their young before heading south to Antarctica.

To get the most out of your journey, consider staying at Bahia Bustamante, an isolated sheep farm with a diversity of wildlife that's been likened to the Galapagos. Or volunteer on a penguin conservation project at the newly established penguin colony in Punta Ninfas.

Penguins at Punta Tombo

Penguin lovers, take note: Punta Tombo is home to the largest colony of Magellanic penguins in South America (around 500,000 at last count). During nesting season (September-March), this rookery becomes a hive of squawking, shuffling seabirds.

The best part about this colony is

> **Penguin lovers, take note: Punta Tombo is home to the largest colony of Magellanic penguins in South America (around 500,000 at last count).**

PATAGONIA

how accessible the penguins are. A wooden boardwalk meanders between their nests, meaning you can get within 6ft (2m) of the birds – the perfect distance for a photo with your new penguin best friend. But the birds and their chicks are particularly vulnerable while nesting, so it's important not to disturb them, and always follow the rules set by the wardens.

The odd history of Gaiman and Trelew

If you thought that the dusty steppe of Argentine Patagonia was home to just gauchos and guanaco, you'd be mistaken. The towns of Gaiman and Trelew in the Chubut province have a unique history: both were settled by Welsh families in the 1860s, who arrived seeking new pastures.

All they found was windswept grasslands, but they stayed, and to this day, around a third of local residents still claim Welsh heritage. For a taste of the region's Welsh flair, spend an afternoon in one of Gaiman's tea houses, decorated with tea towels stitched with the Welsh dragon.

In nearby Trelew, you can go even further back in the history of the region at the Museum of Paleontology Egidio Feruglio. It's home to the remains of *Patagotitan mayorum*, a new species of dinosaur believed to be the largest that ever roamed the planet, but its real attraction is the laboratory window where you can watch paleontologists patiently at work, dusting off the world's history before your eyes.

Peninsula Valdes

Patagonia's Charismatic Penguins

Penguins are among the most beloved bird groups, but most people aren't aware that over half of the 18 species of penguins on earth are listed as threatened. Climate change, pollution, and overfishing impoverish their oceans, while habitat degradation, introduced predators, and human disturbance affect them on land.

The good news: because of their natural charisma, penguins can foster public and political support for conservation, and help protect a wide array of other marine wildlife.

Argentine Patagonia offers several excellent locations to visit penguins, such as Punta Tombo, El Pedral, or San Lorenzo colony. As visitors, we should be aware that these are the most valuable and sensitive places for penguins: the area where they are protecting their eggs and chicks for months.

Penguins need large-scale conservation action because they use vast areas of the ocean to feed, but they also require focused local efforts where they nest and breed on land. The Global Penguin Society conducts a range of activities designed to benefit all penguin species, from on-the-ground data collection to securing protection for breeding and feeding areas. Learn more at www.globalpenguinsociety.org.

***Dr. Pablo Garcia Borboroglu**, President, Global Penguin Society*

> **Because of their natural charisma, penguins can foster public and political support for conservation.**

PATAGONIA

Tierra del Fuego

Associated by most travelers with the ends of the earth – this is the place to pick up a cruise to Antarctica, after all – Tierra del Fuego and the world's southernmost city, Ushuaia, are worth the journey south.

Beagle Channel

History behind bars in Ushuaia

Founded by the British in 1884, Ushuaia started out as a penal colony, housing mass murderers and pirates. Although the prison has long since closed to offenders, the fascinating Museo Maritimo y del Presidio is open to visitors (US $20/$525 ARS).

Ushuaia's doorstep glaciers and lakes

Surrounded on three sides by mountains, Ushuaia offers plenty of day hikes. Starting 4mi (7km) from the center, a three-hour hike winds up to the base of the Martial Glacier, with panoramic views of the Beagle Channel. Equally popular is the two-hour hike to Laguna Esmeralda, a stunning, green glacial lake 12mi (20km) northeast of Ushuaia. Shuttle buses (US $17/$445 ARS) drop you off at the trail.

Penguins on Isla Marillo

Another worthwhile excursion is the resident colony of Magellanic, Gentoo, and king penguins on Isla Martillo, 37mi (60km) east of Ushuaia. Avoid the larger ships and instead take an eight-person sailboat tour (around US $95/$2,490 ARS).

Parque Nacional Tierra del Fuego

Due west from Ushuaia, this is the place for trekking through dramatic, windswept scenery. The crown jewel is the Cerro Guanaco trail, with great views from its 3,172ft (967m) summit. Rent a car and get to the park early to avoid the onslaught of cruise ship passengers.

South to Puerto Williams

Cross the Beagle Channel by speedboat to visit the actual southernmost settlement in the world, Chile's Puerto Williams. Just 9mi (14km) south of Ushuaia, it feels a world away from civilization. Don't be surprised if this ends up being a highlight of your trip.

Voyaging to Antarctica

The ultimate adventure from Ushuaia is to the white continent: Antarctica. For most of us this is a chilly, expensive pipe dream. But luckily, last-minute cruise deals still exist. The best bargains are to be had in January and February, which have more frequent departures; just be prepared to spend up to two weeks waiting to grab that deal.

> **Surrounded on three sides by mountains, Ushuaia offers plenty of day hikes.**

OUTDOOR ADVENTURE

Love to hike? Live to camp? Whether your idea of fun is a white-knuckle ride down a Class IV rapid, a multi-day trek through a cloud forest, or doing underwater somersaults with playful sea lions, Argentina is one big, outrageously scenic playground.

OUTDOOR ADVENTURE

Hiking and Trekking

When it comes to hiking in Argentina, the iconic Fitz Roy trek and glacier hikes on Perito Moreno rightly steal the glory — but the less storied landscapes also offer ample rewards.

El Chalten

In the rugged Northwest, trails lead to ancient ruins, weave through wind-sculpted canyons, and cross dazzling salt pans, while Mendoza draws hard-core trekkers to the world's highest mountain outside the Himalayas: Mount Aconcagua.

Independent hiking in these parts requires planning. Public transportation can be limited, and trails sometimes unmarked and poorly maintained. It's often best to hire a car, and wise to check in with park ranger stations and arrange stays at *refugios* (mountain shelters). Park rangers can supply maps, guides, and updated info.

Salta Province

Framed by soaring Andean peaks, the Northwest delivers numerous day hikes and multi-day expeditions through fantastically shaped canyons. The colonial city of Salta is the local tourist epicenter. Some 116mi (187km) north, the charming wine-growing region of Cafayate is the hub for Valles Calchaquíes, where traditional villages nestle amid the thrusting rock formations of the Quebrada de las Flechas. From Cafayate, a scenic, 3mi (5km) hike leads southwest to the Rio Colorado, home to ancient pictographs and a picturesque waterfall.

Jujuy Province

Just north of the city of Jujuy (75mi/120km north of Salta), the Quebrada de Humahuaca is Northwest Argentina's main calling card. A UNESCO World-Heritage Site, this long gorge blazes with waves of vividly colored rock, stretching north to the Bolivian border. Most tourist attention centers on the spectacular Cerro de Siete Colores, the stratified "Hill of Seven Colors," which you can marvel at on a 90-minute hike (1.8mi/3km) around the perimeter.

Nestled beneath the mountain, Purmamarca is a captivating village despite its steady traffic of visitors, and with its rich indigenous traditions and incredible setting, it's an ideal base for hikes and treks for all levels.

The Yungas

106mi (170km) northeast of Purmamarca, adventurous trekkers and budding botanists head west to Calilegua National Park. Home to portions of the Yungas cloud forest,

> **"** Independent hiking in these parts requires planning. Public transportation can be limited, and trails sometimes unmarked and poorly maintained.

OUTDOOR ADVENTURE

The Yungas

that covers swathes of Peru, Bolivia, and Argentina, its lush biodiversity is a far cry from Salta's arid landscape. Accessed from the town of Libertador General San Martin (6mi/9km away), the park has 14mi (22km) of trails for all abilities, which lead from the Aguas Negras ranger station and allow for close encounters with the park's prolific wildlife inventory: 300 species of bird, including the majestic Andean condor, and 60 mammals, including puma and jaguar.

Novice trails include the short but rewarding Momota and La Herradura trails. If you want to make the heart valves squeak, more arduous hikes include trails to La Lagunita (five hours) and Tataupa (2.5 hours) that descend to the river. Multi-day expeditions can be arranged in Salta and San Salvador de Jujuy and include a three-day trek to Cerro Amarillo (12,205ft/3,720m) or Cerro Hermoso (10,499ft/3,200m).

Mendoza Province

The high Andes to the west of Mendoza city are dominated by Mount Aconcagua, aka "Roof of the Americas," South America's highest mountain. While Aconcagua is more of a long hike than a mountaineering expedition, it's definitely a challenge due to elevation (22,840ft/6,960m), severe weather, and duration (18-21 days). Still, with more than 3,500 people taking on the climb each year, it's a well-traveled trail and very doable if you are in good shape. Bear in mind that most travel insurance policies do not cover climbs over 19,685ft (6,000m).

The "Normal" and "Polish Traverse"' routes to the summit don't require gear or technical expertise, but they're essential for the tougher "Polish Glacier" route, which involves crossing a glacier. For novice hikers who don't have three weeks to spare, tour operators in Mendoza offer a two-day trek below the snow line to base camps and *refugios*, including Confluencia (10,826ft/3,300m).

If you're not up for a long commitment, rewarding day hikes are accessible from Mendoza City. Some 7.5mi (12km) west of town, El Challao is a popular, family-friendly hike. The hike to Cerro Arco (three hours return trip to the summit) provides glorious panoramas of the city.

Less than a three-hour drive from Mendoza, Cerro Penitentes (14,272ft/4,350m), named for its jagged rock formations that resemble penitent monks, can be climbed all year round. While the moderately rated two-day hike (16mi/26km, with an overnight camp at the summit) requires no technical expertise, it does require a high level of fitness and hiking experience.

> " **Novice trails include the short but rewarding Momota and La Herradura trails. If you want to make the heart valves squeak, more arduous hikes include trails to La Lagunita (five hours) and Tataupa (2.5 hours).**

OUTDOOR ADVENTURE

Winter Sports

When you ski or snowboard in Argentina, just invert everything you know about the North American or European winter resort experience – ski season in the Southern Hemisphere runs from June to September.

Cerro Catedral

While infrastructure has improved in the last few years, lifts at some resorts can be brutally slow. But you'll enjoy fewer crowds and lower ticket prices than in North America (US $40-$62/$1,050-$1,625 ARS).

Las Leñas

One of the world's largest ski resorts, with more than 40mi (64km) of runs, there's nothing subdued about Mendoza's flashy, flagship resort. Powder hounds flock here for the extreme backcountry skiing and heli-skiing. The easiest way to get here is to fly from Buenos Aires to Malargue Airport (43mi/70km away), and take one of the frequent buses (2.5 hours). If you're on a budget, more affordable accommodation is available at Los Molles, 11mi (18km) away.

Cerro Catedral

Rising above beautiful Lake Nahuel Huapi just 12mi (20km) from Bariloche, Catedral is much more accessible than Las Leñas. The newly expanded resort features the largest lift-accessed ski terrain in South America, with 53 runs for all levels, along with snowshoeing, cross country skiing, hiking, fishing, and horse riding.

Cerro Bayo

Some 6mi (9km) from the Lake District town of Villa La Angostura, Bayo began as a no-frills locals hill, but has been recast as a boutique ski experience famed for its incredible views into Chile. What it lacks in scale, infrastructure, and amenities, it more than compensates for with its off-beat charm, unpretentious vibe, and diverse terrain.

Cerro Chapelco

Chapelco has invested more in lifts, snowmaking, and amenities than any other Argentine resort, and it shows. With just 22 trails that deliver magnificent views of Volcan Lanín, the park is small, but surprisingly varied. Charming San Martin de los Andes, 12mi (19km) away, makes an excellent base.

Cerro Castor

The southernmost ski resort on the continent, Cerro Castor is accessed from Ushuaia (16mi/26km away) in Tierra del Fuego National Park. Blessed with a longer than average season and fantastic powder, Castor draws a cult crowd with its family-friendly atmosphere and blissfully empty slopes.

> **Rising above beautiful Lake Nahuel Huapi just 12mi (20km) from Bariloche, Catedral is much more accessible than Las Leñas.**

OUTDOOR ADVENTURE

Rafting, Kayaking and Diving

From snorkeling with sea lions on the Patagonian coast to intense whitewater rafting in the Lake District, Argentina offers water sports for all interests and skill sets.

Rafting in Mendoza

Patagonia
A World-Heritage Site, Peninsula Valdes is one of the world's most exciting places for marine life encounters. The self-proclaimed "Scuba Diving Capital of Argentina," Puerto Madryn offers whale watching, scuba and wreck diving, and snorkel trips. Full day whale-watching excursions cost US $30-$100 ($786-2,620 ARS), depending on locations visited.

Scuba diving with sea lions at Punta Loma (11mi/17km south) includes 45 minutes of hanging out on the sea floor with gregarious pups, plus instruction on how to interact with them. Tours generally include all rental equipment and round-trip transportation.

About 62mi (100km) west of Puerto Madryn, Puerto Piramides is the base for sea kayaking, with outfitters on Avenida de las Ballenas offering half-day (US $70/$1,835 ARS), full-day (US $120/$3,145 ARS) and multi-day trips geared to beginners and intermediates.

The Lake District
Bariloche is a wonderful base for whitewater rafting in Nahuel Huapi National Park. Rafting season along the Rio Manso runs from mid October to early May – local outfitters offer everything from day trips (from US $80/$2,095 ARS) to week-long expeditions (US $1,600/$41,920 ARS). The relatively gentle Manso Clasico (Class II-III) begins at Steffen Lake. For white-knuckle thrills, the Manso de la Frontera (Class IV) trip passes through breathtaking Velvet Canyon and ends near the Chilean border.

Half-day kayaking and paddleboard trips on Lake Gutierrez also depart from Bariloche.

Mendoza Province
Within striking distance of the city, the churning waters of the Mendoza and Diamante Rivers lure adventure sport enthusiasts. Whitewater rafting trips are offered year round. Most people visit the rafting mecca of Potrerillos (32mi/51km west of Mendoza) on a day trip from the city. Trips range from half- and full-day trips (US $37/90 or $970/2,360 ARS) to two-day, Class III-IV excursions. Experience isn't a prerequisite, but strongly advised for anything above Class II.

> Within striking distance of the city, the churning waters of the Mendoza and Diamante Rivers lure adventure sport enthusiasts.

OUTDOOR ADVENTURE

Camping

Camping is a big part of the Argentine national identity. Campgrounds are extremely busy during high season: booking ahead is highly recommended.

Prices noted here are per person and discounts for longer stays will apply.

Patagonia

Private, municipal, wild, and free camping

Most of Argentina's national parks are dotted with campsites of the Camping Libre ilk, which, as the name suggests, are free of charge and facilities; often just a latrine – but your reward is unspoiled scenery and solitude.

Municipal sites also have limited amenities, but they're generally well maintained and equipped with *fogones* (open fire grills). Private campsites rival the best in Europe and North America, with lots of amenities. For a truly rustic experience, you can generally pitch your tent anywhere on public land. Wherever you camp, be sure to remove all trash.

Camping gear

Weather in Argentina changes fast, and smart packing is critical. If you don't have your own gear, you can hire what you need from camping stores or outfitters in adventure travel hubs.

Salta and the northwest

In Salta, Camping Municipal Carlos Xamena offers easy town access and amenities galore (US $3/$79 ARS per night). In Cafayate, Camping Luz y Fuerza is a convenient base for day hikes within the Northwest's polychromatic canyons (US $2/$53 ARS per night).

Patagonia

Some 32mi (52km) from El Calafate, within Los Glaciares National Park, the private Lago Roca Campsite raises the bar with excellent camping facilities, well-equipped cabins, hot showers, and a restaurant.

El Chalten is one of the top trekking centers in Argentina, and there are three free campsites within a 90-minute walk (6mi/10km) of town: Campamento Poincenot, Campamento Laguna Capri, and Padre D'Agostini. Laguna Capri offers the best views.

The Lake District

Lago Gutierrez has unusually warm waters, perfect for swimming, and a well-equipped private campsite right on the lake.

Some 11mi (18km) from El Bolson, Kumelen offers fully equipped cabins (US $70/$1,835 ARS), nice dorms (US $7/$185 ARS), or camping (US $9/$235 ARS), all with access to clean bathrooms with hot water and a communal kitchen.

> "El Chalten is one of the top trekking centers in Argentina, and there are three free campsites within a 90-minute walk (6mi/10km) of town."

OUTDOOR ADVENTURE

Where to See Wildlife

With ecosystems ranging from austere steppe to subtropical jungle, Argentina is home to a huge diversity of flora and fauna. While Patagonia and Iguazu National Park are the best known areas for wildlife viewing, the Yungas, El Chaco, and Pampa de Achala regions offer an equally rewarding (and often more intimate) experience.

Condor

The Yungas

The arid landscapes around Salta are a world apart from the cloud and montane forests that comprise the Yungas. Parque Nacional Calilegua is one of Argentina's most biologically diverse ecosystems, with more than 270 identified animal species, including 50 per cent of all bird species in the country. But you'll have to get seriously deep in the forest (and be very lucky) to catch a glimpse of the park's resident mammals, which include jaguar, ocelot, puma, monkeys, otters, peccaries, and tapir.

Guided tours are available from Salta and San Salvador de Jujuy, and a trained guide will greatly improve your chances of spotting the park's elusive mammals. Calilegua is massive, so spending a night at the Aguas Negras campsite is recommended. Independent travelers can access the park from San Salvador de Jujuy (75mi or 120km) and from Salta (106mi or 170km). There are regular bus services from Salta to Libertador General San Martin (6mi or 9km away), and then from Libertador to San Francisco, within the park.

In the center of Salta Province, Parque Nacional El Rey preserves another remarkable tranche of Yungas cloud forest. The park's biodiversity is impressive, with 21 species of reptiles, 255 species of birds, and 50 species of mammals. Located 125mi (200km) from Salta, tour operators offer 4x4 day tours for around US $250 ($6,560 ARS), with the focus on hiking and wildlife watching.

El Baritu National Park is the least accessible of the northwest's national parks, requiring a stop in Bolivia to reach Aguas Blancas and Los Toldos, the regional gateways. For hard-core wildlife enthusiasts, it's worth the trek.

Pampa de Achala

Named for the park's poster child, the Andean condor, Quebrada del

> **Named for the park's poster child, the Andean condor, Quebrada del Condorito National Park undulates across the high peaks of the Sierras de Cordoba.**

46

Condorito National Park undulates across the high peaks of the Sierras de Cordoba. Accessible year-round, the park's canyons are prime condor nesting sites, and can be visited with little effort from Villa Carlos Paz (34mi or 55km), or Cordoba (56mi or 90km). Most travelers take the moderately rated, 6mi (9km) Senda a La Quebrada del Condorito, a marked hiking trail which descends to Balcon Norte, a lookout point where young condors hone their flight skills at what is known as the *Escuela de Vuelo* (Flight School).

The park is also home to less-conspicuous mammals, including puma and red fox, as well as more visible snakes, lizards, and geckos; be mindful of the park's venomous snakes, namely the big yarara. The birdlife is prolific – in addition to condors, you may see grey-hooded parakeets, Magellanic woodpeckers, and the protected grey-hooded sierra finch. Most travelers sign up for a tour from Cordoba, but independent travelers can take a bus from Cordoba to the park's entrance at La Pampilla (about 1.5 hours; direction Mina Clavero).

El Gran Chaco

Located in one of Argentina's poorest regions, there's no shortage of superlatives to describe Gran Chaco. Covering vast swathes of Argentina, Paraguay, Bolivia, and Brazil, the Chaco contains the second-largest forest on the continent and ranks as the largest dry forest in South America. What the Gran Chaco lacks in scenic majesty it more than makes up for in biodiversity,

Maned wolf

with a wildlife inventory that includes jaguar, maned wolf, puma, anteaters, and the world's largest armadillo. Birders will be in their element, with over 500 species logged in the Chaco's dry region.

Human influence here has been minimal, and the few travelers that venture here generally do so on a guided tour; most of the Chaco is inaccessible, with poor transport links and horrendous roads. The region's most accessible national parks are Parque Nacional Chaco (reached from Resistencia), and Parque Nacional Río Pilcomayo (reached from Formosa)

In the center of the Chaco region, El Impenetrable – Argentina's newest national park – offers spectacular bird and animal life. The park's wetter regions are a haven for capybara, two species of caiman, and tapir. Park facilities are non-existent and (at the time of writing) there is no accommodation close to the park. Independent travelers can access the park at Paraje La Armonia (37mi or 60km from Miraflores), which is linked by bus service from Miraflores to Nueva Pompeya.

> **What the Gran Chaco lacks in scenic majesty it more than makes up for in biodiversity, with a wildlife inventory that includes jaguar, maned wolf, puma, anteaters, and the world's largest armadillo.**

OUTDOOR ADVENTURE

Best Road Trips

Argentina is an incredibly diverse country with endless things to see and do — but it's also a very large country. To make the most of it, your best bet is to choose a region (or two), rent a car and road-trip around.

Having your own wheels is the ultimate in travel freedom, and is the absolute best way to find hidden gems and off-track spots. Unless you plan to do a full "loop" during your Argentina travels, it's best to rent and return from the same place to save the hefty drop-off fee.

Quebrada de las Flechas

Salta and Jujuy itinerary

These two provinces are unlike anywhere else in the country. Located in the Northwest and bordered by Chile, Paraguay, and Bolivia, everything has a traditional feeling here, including clothing, music, and food. Before the Spanish conquest, this area was inhabited by indigenous tribes, including the Quilmes and Humahuacas. Fun facts: Quilmes is the name of a popular beer in Argentina, and Quebradas de Humahuaca is one of the most stunning drives in the area.

Suggested route: Salta (a few days), Cafayate (a few days), Cachi (one night), Tilcara (a few days), Salinas Grandes (day trip from Tilcara), Purmamarca (day trip from Tilcara), Salta (finish).

Highlights of this area include:
- Museums, architecture, parks, plazas, and restaurants in Salta City
- Quebradas de las Conchas National Park on the drive from Salta to Cafayate
- The amazing wineries surrounding Cafayate (don't miss Bad Brothers, El Esteco, and Piattelli Vineyards)
- Quebrada de las Flechas (jagged rock formations)
- Old Route 9 with lush green scenery, rivers, and gorges
- The traditional feel and food in Tilcara (try the llama!)
- The colourful mountains in Purmamarca (best seen at dawn)
- The blindingly white Salinas Grandes (salt flats).

Mendoza itinerary

Mendoza is most famous for its acclaimed wineries surrounded by Andean peaks, but there's plenty to do in the area that doesn't involve grapes.

> **Located in the Northwest and bordered by Chile, Paraguay, and Bolivia, everything has a traditional feeling here, including clothing, music, and food.**

OUTDOOR ADVENTURE

The city is actually a university town with lots of lively bars and restaurants attracting a younger crowd.

During your trip to Mendoza, we suggest driving out to the famous wineries of Norton, Ruca Malen, and Trapiche for lunch and wine (but just a glass, you're driving!).

Then, drive to Aconcagua (22,840ft/6960m) the tallest mountain outside of Asia and the highest peak in the southern hemisphere.

A 120mi (193km) drive through twisty mountain roads will bring you to the Aconcagua Provincial Park. A US $20 ($525 ARS) pass gives you you access all the way up to the Base Camp (a six-hour return hike). Or, for a mere US $1.30 ($34 ARS), you can access the park up until the trailhead, which allows you about two hours of hiking.

Finally, after you've eaten, sipped, and hiked your way around Mendoza, it's time to relax. Drive out to the Termas Cacheuta, about 90 minutes from town. Enjoy the thermal springs in stone pools with views of the Andes – there's also a spa and restaurant.

Note: if you want to drive your rental car over the border from Argentina into Chile, you'll need written permission from the rental company and the proper insurance to do so. Speak to the car rental agent before attempting to cross, or you'll be turned away if you don't have the correct documents.

Lake District itinerary

Patagonia's Lake District is just that – a district of gorgeous lakes. It's an incredibly scenic area, and the perfect destination to explore by car.

There are many routes you can take, but here's our suggested itinerary: Bariloche (a few days), Circuito Chico (day trip from Bariloche), Limay River (day trip from Bariloche), Villa La Angostura (a few days), San Martin de los Andes (a few days), Lake Lolog (day trip from San Martín de los Andes), Bariloche (finish)

Highlights of this road trip include:
- Bariloche, offering views of the Andes Mountains, the Circuito Chico drive with hiking and lakes to explore, and great restaurants (try Alto el Fuego)
- Fly fishing on the Limay River
- Hiking around Lake Nahuel Huapi and Correntoso Lake in Villa La Angostura
- Lanin National Park outside of San Martin de los Andes
- Fly fishing and a picnic at Lake Lolog
- Wandering the pretty streets of San Martin de los Andes.

Aconcagua

Packing for a Road Trip

Many areas of Argentina are desert, and you'll often find yourself in the middle of nowhere – which is a good thing, if you're properly prepared. This means having a full tank of gas, first-aid kit, a spare tire, tools, a map, data plan on your phone, a Spanish translation app or phrasebook, plus non-perishable food and drinking water.

OUTDOOR ADVENTURE

Off the Beaten Path

Argentina's vast territory hides many secret treasures. From a lost village, to a moon-like volcanic plain, to a prehistoric lagoon, here are four worth going out of your way for.

Barreal Blanco

Yavi and Yavi Chico, Jujuy Province

Over 11,280ft (3,440m) above sea level, Yavi stands frozen in time, its arid Andean landscapes contrasting with the willow trees that grow by the river and the houses made of clay.

Located near the Bolivian border, 2.5 hours from the backpacker's haven of Humahuaca, this barely populated village is the last town in Argentina that belonged to the Royal Road. During the days of Spanish rule, precious minerals were transported through here from Peru, making Yavi a powerful marquisate.

Visitors can check out the Marques de Tojo's elegant colonial-style house, now a museum, and the 17th-century church with its gold-plated altar.

A short hike takes you to even smaller Yavi Chico, which has an archeological museum and – along the river – cave paintings that date back centuries.

For those who wish to stay, there's a municipal campsite just by the Marques' house, or the Hostal de Yavi.

Barreal Blanco, aka "Pampa el Leoncito," San Juan Province

In prehistoric times, the Barreal Blanco was a lagoon. Today, it's a 9mi (15km) long, 3mi (5km) wide expanse of flat, white, dry soil with no vegetation at all and winds that blow at more than 75mph (120kph).

This unique feature makes Barreal Blanco the perfect spot for "land-sailing" – an adrenaline-producing, unconventional sport like windsurfing, but on land. Even if you try to stand still, the wind will take you. You can book the experience locally, or bring your own "carro."

Just 11mi (17km) from the Barreal Blanco is the Complejo Astronomico El Leoncito. This astronomical observatory can be visited on a guided tour – it's also possible to spend the night if you book in advance. This particular spot has 300 clear nights a year and no light pollution, so sightings of the Milky Way are guaranteed. There's another observatory nearby, the Observatorio

> **In prehistoric times, the Barreal Blanco was a lagoon. Today, it's a 9mi (15km) long, 3mi (5km) wide expanse of flat, white, dry soil with no vegetation at all.**

OUTDOOR ADVENTURE

Astronomico U. CESCO, that can also be visited.

As this area is part of the Leoncito National Park, it's best accessed from the nearest town, Barreal.

Parque Nacional Sierra de las Quijadas, San Luis Province

Though few travelers know about this national park, it has a very rich cultural and palaeontological heritage. It was once home of the Huarpes Tribe and, long before, of the pterodaustro; a dinosaur species that hasn't been found anywhere else.

The park's extremely arid landscape and dramatic rock formations resemble the Grand Canyon. Temperatures can rise up to more than 99°F (37°C) – some of the activities within the park may be suspended when this happens, and during summer months hikes are generally not held during siesta hours.

The main features of the park are the Potrero de la Aguada (a natural amphitheater carved by wind and water) and Farallones (walls of red sandstone over 656ft/200m high). Explorers can do some hikes, such as the Guanacos trail, on their own, but must register at the park's office beforehand. Other hikes, like the Farallones (four hours) or Las Huellas del Pasado (two hours) require a guide.

This is quite an isolated area, and there's no public transport, so make sure you are stocked with plenty of water, food, and proper clothing (and a full gas tank if driving). There is a basic camping and recreation area nearby.

La Payunia

Travelers usually visit for the day from the main towns nearby, like Merlo or Lujan.

Reserva Provincial La Payunia, Mendoza

The Pampa Negra was formed by more than 800 volcanic cones, turning it into a black desert. This moon-like landscape has one of the highest and most varied concentrations of volcanic activity on earth. Still an off-the-beaten-path destination, La Payunia can only be visited in the company of an authorized guide.

Travelers can either hire a guide to join them and self-drive, or do a day trip with a tour operator. This is to preserve the solitude of this volcanic wonderland and to prevent people from getting lost or getting their vehicle stuck in the soft black sand. If you self-drive, you'll need an SUV.

All guided tours depart from Malargue, 93mi (150km) away. There's no accommodation nearby and the visit lasts the whole day, so you only need to sit back and enjoy the ride.

> ❝ This moon-like landscape has one of the highest and most varied concentrations of volcanic activity on earth.

Essential Insurance Tips

If you're heading to Argentina, chances are that you'll be skiing, snowboarding, or hiking. And while you're wandering the streets, you may experience petty crime. We've created this guide to help you navigate travel insurance, so you can make the most of your trip.

BAGGAGE
Cash

The theft of cash is common in Argentina, so it's important that you know where your insurance cover does and doesn't apply – especially if you're the type of traveler who takes out large amounts of money to avoid international transaction fees.

First up, there's no cover for stolen cash for American, Brazilian, or Canadian travelers. You can't add it on to the policy as an extra, either.

Secondly, for all other travelers where there is cover, you'll need to buy the Explorer plan, and an excess will apply. An excess means that we'll deduct a certain amount (which your policy will specify) from your claim before you're paid out.

Lastly, there are also conditions of cover that vary from policy to policy. For example, most policies require you to actually witness your cash being stolen in order for it to be covered. We're well aware that pickpocketing occurs and is an unfortunate part of traveling, however if you're carrying cash and you don't see it get stolen, the line between loss and theft gets blurred – and policies don't cover loss of cash.

There is also cover for stolen cash if it's been taken from a locked safe and there's evidence of damage or forced entry. Keeping your money in a safe shows that you've done everything in your power to keep the cash safe. And of course, forced entry helps validate your claim.

If your cash is stolen, you must report it to the police as soon as possible, and get something in writing from them. We know that language, corruption, and straight-out indifference can be a barrier to police assistance in some countries, but our insurance partners require certain documentation to validate and process claims.

Passports

Having your passport stolen overseas can strike fear into the most seasoned traveler. While your mum can send you money if your credit card is stolen, or you can borrow a friend's bra after the laundromat attendant says "what clothes?", replacing your passport isn't so easy to do.

Our 24/7 emergency assistance teams can give you advice on what to do if your passport is stolen, and direct you to the nearest consulate to get a replacement. However, not all policies cover emergency replacement passports. There's no cover for US or Brazilian residents, but for everyone

> **Having your passport stolen overseas can strike fear into the most seasoned traveler.**

Travel insurance isn't designed to cover everything, so take the time to read the full description of cover in your policy wording, so you'll know exactly what is and isn't covered.

else, our travel insurance policies can cover your emergency replacement passport expenses.

The good news for Americans, Brits, and Irish, is that cover applies for additional expenses incurred while you're delayed as a result of a stolen passport, such as the cost of additional meals and local transport.

As with stolen cash, you'll need to report the theft to the police as soon as possible and get something in writing from them.

What is an excess and why is it there?

A policy excess (also known as a deductible) is the amount that you're required to contribute towards your claim before your policy kicks in. Most travel insurance policies come with an excess, which will be deducted from your claim if it's successful. If your claim is less than the excess, then you don't get paid out. If your claim isn't successful, you're not required to pay the excess.

The reason travel insurance policies have an excess is to keep the premium down. This is done by eliminating many of the smaller claims. While that might seem unfair, it also means that the premium is more affordable for bigger claims, such as overseas medical or bringing you home for further treatment if you're sick or injured.

ACTIVITIES

travel insurance policies are designed so you can choose the right policy for the

Skiing in Patagonia

activities you're doing, giving you access to the help you need when you need it.

If you visit our helpdesk, or read through the activities section of the purchase path, you'll be able to see the level of cover that you'll need. All plans are different and may require an upgrade for certain activities. Read the policy wording carefully to choose the right plan and/or adventure sport option for your trip.

Skiing & Snowboarding

Argentina's slopes provide ample opportunity to hone your skills. Big dumps, fresh tracks and bluebird days will make for an epic trip, yet accidents on and off the hill do happen, even to the most experienced sliders. All of our insurers cover skiing and snowboarding, though not all policies do, so make sure you select the correct policy for your ski trip at the time of purchase.

When you get a quote online, you'll see that there's a list of sports and activities with the corresponding level of cover next to it. Read this list carefully so you know if you need to upgrade your policy at the time of purchase. It's worth remembering that you can't upgrade a policy once you've bought it. So, if you buy a policy without the correct cover for skiing or snowboarding, and the policy has started or is outside of the free-look period, you'll need to buy an additional policy for the time you're on the slopes in Argentina (or anywhere else for that matter!). And, as you've traveled on your policy, you won't be able to get a refund for the duplicate.

Provided you've selected and bought the correct policy, you're not putting yourself needlessly at risk, and you're adhering to the policy terms and conditions, if you tear an ACL or MCL, pop a knee, or are involved in any other injury as a result of skiing or snowboarding, the policy covers medivac including ski patrol, hospitalization, outpatient treatment and other medical expenses. You can read more here.

Hiking

Apart from planning for the weather (and packing correctly), you'll need to know the altitude that you'll be hiking/trekking to in Argentina, so you can buy the correct level of coverage at the time of purchase. Many parts of Argentina are thinly populated and remote, which can make it difficult to get help if you don't have insurance. If you get altitude sickness or you're injured on the mountain and don't have the right insurance, or any insurance for that matter, a heli-evac to get you to medical care can be very expensive.

If you do get injured in the mountains, it's essential that you get in touch with our emergency assistance teams straight away, so that they can support you from the time you fall sick or get injured, until the time you recover. They'll be able to help you get to the nearest hospital, if you need it, and get you home, if required, so that you can get the ongoing medical care that you need.

However, once you're home, cover stops, so you'll need to have access to government health care or your own private medical insurance for those costs.

> Weather conditions can change quickly, so make sure you're prepared. Search and rescue isn't covered in any of our policies, so make sure you know where you are at all times.

Notes

Notes

Notes

Notes

Notes

Notes

Notes

Notes

Notes

Notes

Notes

Notes

Notes

Notes

Notes

Notes

Notes

Notes

Printed in Great Britain
by Amazon